Huddersfield
A Third Selection
IN OLD PHOTOGRAPHS

The people here at Huddersfield are so hospitable, that there is hardly anything they wont do, to ensure one having a good time.

Manners maketh the man – in Huddersfield!

Huddersfield

A Third Selection

IN OLD PHOTOGRAPHS

HAZEL WHEELER

Alan Sutton Publishing Limited
Phoenix Mill · Far Thrupp · Stroud
Gloucestershire

First Published 1994

Copyright © Hazel Wheeler, 1994

British Library Cataloguing in Publication Data.
A catalogue record for this book is available from
the British Library.

ISBN 0–7509–0707–X

Typeset in 9/10 Sabon.
Typesetting and origination by
Alan Sutton Publishing Limited.
Printed in Great Britain by
Redwood Books, Trowbridge.

Contents

Introduction

Huddersfield people derive a great deal of amusement from looking back on the past of their town. Of particular delight are fiascos, such as that time in the 1950s when Isobel Baillie, a famous soprano, was singing at Golcar Baptist church with Walter Widdop. As they neared the close of a glorious aria from Haydn's *Creation*, all of the lights fused. Fortunately a girl in the choir had a torch, and shone it for the organist, who continued undaunted. But Huddersfield's history is made up of more than fiascos.

Before the Wembley Exhibition of 1924 the Clayton West Co-op placed a big jar of dried peas in a window. Anyone paying a penny was allowed to guess how many there were. George Gray guessed 963 – the nearest – and was awarded a free ticket to Wembley. On 23 April that year crowds gathered in Greenhead Park to hear the broadcast of the King's Speech in Wembley relayed. All dressed up for the event, the people's heads bowed reverently through a prayer. Some schoolchildren were taken on a visit to Wembley, under the charge of Huddersfield schoolteachers.

The 1920s is still a period of great interest, being within living memory for some but an unknown era for most. Huddersfield has changed vastly. For instance, an advert of 13 February 1924 read: 'Will the person who took the moleskin muff from the Princess Picture House please return it to the management.' And on 23 February: 'Miss Reeve offers 150 children's dresses at 10s 6d and 21s, 15, Cloth Hall Street.'

Ups and downs in personal relationships resulted in some lively court hearings. Tom Stringer was summoned by his wife Mary Ellen for aggravated assault. Before proceedings began a previous separation order, granted on the grounds of persistent cruelty, was annulled, as cohabitation had been resumed.

Mr T. Smailes, appearing for the complainant, stated that one day the defendant had kicked her on the leg. Then, when she fell to the floor, he kicked her on the head and both legs. The defendant told the court that life was unbearable with his wife: she had a violent temper and threw things at him. On the day of the alleged assault she had called his mother an offensive name. When he ran towards her she went outside and fell between a horse's legs.

An order was granted: the defendant was to contribute 20s a week towards his wife's maintenance, to pay costs, and a penalty of 5s was imposed on account of the assault. The defendant asked how long a sentence he would receive for default. The magistrate's clerk told him six days. 'Well, I'm ready for going down', was the reply.

Crime is ever present, in different guises. In September 1924, for example, a number of counterfeit florins were circulating in the town. Meanwhile a different way of stealing, at the Picturedrome, starred Rudolph Valentino in *Stolen Moments*. The Princess Picture House and Café held supper dances every Saturday for 2s and afternoon tea dances every Wednesday for a 1s 6d entrance fee.

Huddersfield in the 1920s danced to a very different tempo. New dance records from J. Wood & Sons of No. 67 New Street included 'The Vamp' (an oriental foxtrot), 'Joy Bells of Peace' (a waltz), 'Tango Bonita', and the foxtrot 'How ya gonna keep 'em, down on the farm . . .'. And everyone seemed to be an expert on the Charleston, even in Huddersfield.

In 1920 a lady lost a black fur on leaving the second house of the Hippodrome. Perhaps more inconveniently, the top set of a pair of false teeth was lost on a tramcar from Huddersfield to Slaithwaite. It being a Saturday night, maybe the distraught owner, who offered a reward if it was returned to the police station, was drunk. Quite a number of velour hats were mislaid that winter, too.

As for the cost of clothes, Rushworth's sale price corsets were 8s 11d, and Kahns were selling ladies' coats with fur collars, usually around £4 10s, for 52s 6d and navy cashmere mackintoshes from 25s.

In late November 1926, Whiteley's, the confectioners of Market Walk, let it be known that its 'Gay Xmas Show is open for Inspection'.

Do you remember being given one of those boring boxes of handkerchiefs for Christmas? Rushworth's had 'Pure Irish linen, 6 lovely embroidered designs in a pretty box, 10s 6d'. Snowdon's in Kirkgate had chocolate figures, Christmas stockings and Crawford tartan shortbread – 'Delightful for afternoon tea'. Meadow Dairy was selling 'Fine large eggs, preserved, 1¾ each'. Customers were advised to get in a good supply at the low price.

George Hall's Toyland was the place to go for children in 1926:

Here, amongst the bright festoons and gay coloured lights, discover with cries of delight – wonderful mechanical toys that do unexpected things; motors, clowns, railway sets, aeroplanes and signal outfits, fire engines; big dolls and dolls houses, prams, blackboards, housekeeping sets, and stacks of housewifely things.

That year there was a 'Boots for Bairns Fund' distribution by the Cinderella Society. Some poor youngsters would have had no Christmas fare without charity such as that.

Rushworth's sold outfits for juvenile parties: jap silk with frills and imitation lace at 6s 11d to 29s 6d; knickers to match for 4s 6d to 16s 11d. Also taffeta, georgette, crêpe de Chine and satin from 22s 6d to six guineas. Before there was central heating in the majority of houses, wearing a party dress on Christmas Day meant that a warm liberty bodice had to be worn underneath, or one would have been unbearably cold.

In 1920 a cook-general was required for a house in Gledholt: £50 a year, with plenty of liberty. (I bet that wouldn't have bought many liberty bodices!)

A group of Deighton chapel members on a trip to the seaside in the 1930s. Hazel Taylor (the author) is on the far left next to Lena Medley. Hilda Taylor is on the right, wearing a fur collar, and Philip Taylor (the author's brother) is on the far right.

Fred Wood of No. 56 John William Street could clean and block one's velour hat in seven days for 3s. Mr W. Matheson was plying his dentistry at No. 7 Chapel Hill. Gilbert Vizard of No. 20 Queen Street was a rupture specialist and maker of artificial limbs, abdominal belts, etc. A. Strange, a hairdresser, was opposite the tramway offices at the top of Northumberland Street. From 25 July 1920 the Sunday tram service was to commence at 3.00 p.m. and run for an hour longer than previously.

Girls were wanted for the laundry-packing department of J. Holroyd & Co., Seed Hill, and in Milnsbridge a family of three sought to 'put out washing, good price paid'. R.J. Elliott & Co., the cigar makers, required young girls aged 13–14 to learn 'cigar making and stripping'. Jennings' College, at the top of King Street, guaranteed proficiency in cases of neglected education. 'Backward Youths and Young Ladies could attend daily.'

Complaints were made that the rent for corporation allotments had been raised from 2s 6d to 4s. However, there was always Prince Royal snuff to be bought when life went a bit awry: 'Clears the head and brightens the brain'.

In readiness for Easter 1927 the Public Benefit Co. at No. 4 King Street and No. 6 Cross Church Street sold shoes for children from 6s 11d, including tan glacé kid shoes. Miss Greenwood at No. 13 Victoria Street was noted for exquisite pure silk hose for 2s 11½d, 3s 11½d, 4s 6d and upwards. Brough's of No. 6 Kirkgate had cherry slab cake at 8d/lb, rich Genoa at 10d/lb and sultana at 8d/lb. Slab cake was all the rage at teatime, after a bit of Hovis bread or Bermaline, a brown loaf with a paper wrapper round the middle.

Special half-day excursions to Skegness that season cost 6s. On 9 April Huddersfield's New Hippodrome and Opera House featured Jack Hylton and his world-famous band. Royal stalls were 3s, grand circle 2s 6d, stalls 1s 6d, circle 1s 6d and balcony 6d. Maybe some enjoying the show were wearing the newest wrap-round corsets from Wakefield's of No. 18 Cross Church Street, which cost from 3s 11½d to 25s.

Marjorie Williams (later Mrs Stanley), who was born at Blackhouse Road, Fartown, remembers her mother, Hilda, baking bread at 5.00 a.m. during summer so that the coal fire didn't have to be stoked up so high in the heat of the day. Extra grubby clothes were scrubbed on a metal rubbing board, and what a treat it was to see the results of such hard labour blowing on the rope clothes line in the fresh air.

Breakfast was often dripping on bread. Hilda concocted many a tasty dinner out of sixpennyworth of liver and heart from the butcher Alan Balmforth – more gravy than meat. This was followed by sago, tapioca or rice pudding, cooked slowly in the oven. These were enticing, homely, inexpensive dinners, to greet Marjorie and her sisters on their return from Woodhouse School at midday.

Good manners were not restricted to the rich. It was a strict rule that the children said 'Please', 'Thank you' and 'Please may I leave the table?' when plates were empty. Coats for the girls were made from the best parts of outgrown or outworn adult coats. Mrs Williams sat up through the night one Easter Eve to have one ready for the next day.

Marjorie first worked at L.B. Holliday's. She walked to work daily, trudging through deep snowdrifts in winter across the Ridings to get there for 8.00 a.m. Kitty, the boss, jollied the packing of dyes along by whistling – tunes of the 1920s and with two fingers in her mouth. One day Marjorie took a sample dye home and dyed a pair of artificial silk stockings pink!

Marjorie recalls childhood Christmasses. To prolong the excitement Isaac, her father, hid presents in odd places. One year Marjorie found a mouth organ in the mangle, a little book in the boiler and a penny behind a chair.

From momentous civic events to simple family life, all are illustrated within these pages.

SECTION ONE

The Town

King Street, 1905. At the top of the building on the corner was Jennings' College, School of Shorthand, with the *Yorkshire Daily Observer* newspaper offices below it. Even schoolboys dressed smartly to go into town then (such as the one with what appears to be a drum, on the right).

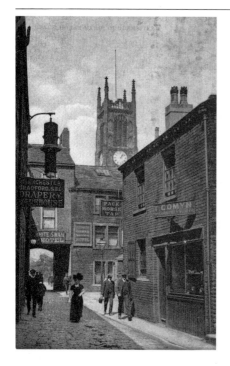

Pack Horse Yard. Such a lot of Huddersfield's character disappeared when this yard, with its cobbled area and fascinating little shops, made way for the modern precinct. Passing the Pack Horse Hotel one could often detect the smell of beer and of dinner cooking. The Manchester and Bradford Drapery Warehouse is on the left and T. Comyn, watchmaker and jeweller, is on the right.

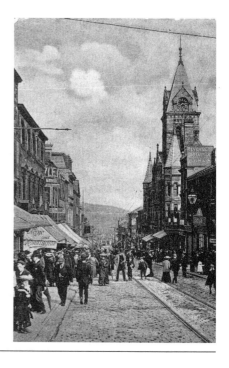

Christmas shopping in King Street, 1904. Kaye and Monnington, later Kaye's, is on the left, and the New Inn is farther down the street. On the right, in front of the market clock, was the Devonshire Restaurant and the YMCA. Just round the corner the Kingsway Café was a popular meeting-place in later years.

The bustling market-place, 1904. The Waverley Hotel is on the left, over the Scotch Bakery. Freeman, Hardy & Willis, the shoe shop, is opposite. Jones' sewing-machine shop is on the right. A cool refreshing drink of water was always available from the fountain in the centre.

John William Street in the early 1900s. George Field, a top-class outfitter, is on the left, and Bellarby's confectioner's cart is drawn up outside. The Huddersfield Building Society is on the left in the distance, on the corner of St George's Square.

Buxton Road at the opposite end of town. The Picture Palace, on the left, had continuous performances between 2.30 p.m. and 10.30 p.m. It later became the Picturedrome, then the Curzon in the 1950s. Harry Roebuck, a fine art dealer, is to the left of the Picture Palace.

Central Co-operative Stores, Buxton Road. The millinery department is to the left of the door. The Co-op incorporated the Victoria Hall and Tea Rooms. Field's coffee is advertised on top of the tram, which is bound for Crosland Moor.

The tram for Moldgreen, King Street. George Hall's is on the left, below the market hall. Hilton's shoe shop is on the right and the New Inn is next door.

Market Walk. A hotel is on the left, and a watchmaker and jewellers is next door. If only the gossiping ladies grouped on the right could come alive, so that we could hear the news of the day.

Cross Church Street. On the left, by the ladder, is Freeman, Hardy & Willis. The White Lion Hotel is opposite.

The Hippodrome, 1914. This was formerly the Armoury, and was converted to a theatre in 1905 and opened by Vesta Tilley. In 1926 there were plays on in the summer and musicals in the winter season. In 1930 the building was converted to the Tudor Cinema. Remember queuing to see a picture, especially on Saturday nights? Rain or snow, it didn't matter – camaraderie in the queue was part of the night out. The cinema later became the Essoldo and was destroyed by fire in 1967.

New Street, 1911. The No. 11 tram for Longwood advertises Field's coffee, Westgate. One would need a cup of that gorgeous beverage after a ride on top of the open tramcar in winter time! King, Walshaw & Co., the chemist, is opposite. Next door is a printers, now Wheatley Dyson's.

Westgate, 1915. Whiteley's Café is on the left, Cooper & Webb further down the street and the Plough Inn is on the right. Without exception all of the gentlemen appear smartly dressed. What a shock they would have if they could witness the sights of Huddersfield eighty years on.

John William Street. In 1920 'Herbert' wrote on this card: 'This is one of our streets in Huddersfield, not very interesting eh. The building marked with an X is my club. My tramcar goes from the bottom right-hand corner.' The No. 4 tram for Marsden was on its way.

Cloth Hall Street. In 1930 J. Cuttell, a tea and coffee specialist, traded at the top of this street, exhorting customers to buy Empire produce. Above was Fred Lee, incorporated accountant, and H. & H. Walker, high-class tailors and costumiers. King's Head Buildings and arcade were opposite, next to the White Hart Hotel. Barrett's carpet and furniture store can just be made out at the bottom of the street, on the corner of New Street. Balmoral Studios is on the right, with F. Chappell, auctioneer and valuer, above.

New Street, 1936. Dunn & Co., hat makers, is on the right. It closed down in 1991. The No. 4 tram for Bradley is passing. On the right side of the road, from left to right, are Marks & Spencer, Dr Scholl's Foot Comfort Service, True Form shoes, Stylo and Dunns. Facing King Street, across the road, is the National Provincial Bank. Timothy, White & Taylor, the chemist, was on the left at the top of the street.

John William Street in the late 1950s. On the right is Henry's store, which was destroyed by fire. Burton's, 'The Tailor of Taste', is next door. Rushworth's, on the left, was still one of the smartest shops in town, and next to it was W.H. Smith's.

Shambles Lane, 1950. Bright bunches of yellow mimosa were sold outside Lindon Smith's in January, heralding the spring. Assistants in fingerless gloves cheerfully attended to customers in bitterly cold weather, muffled against the elements in scarves and thick waistcoats. After going to the pictures, it was common for people to round off the evening with fish and chips in Lindon Smith's café, on the right. The Maypole grocers is facing Shambles Lane. The Unicorn Public House is on the corner, on the right.

Friday afternoon in Huddersfield Market, a painting of the old market. Here one could buy everything and meet everybody beneath the domed splendour of this cherished old building.

SECTION TWO

Hospitals

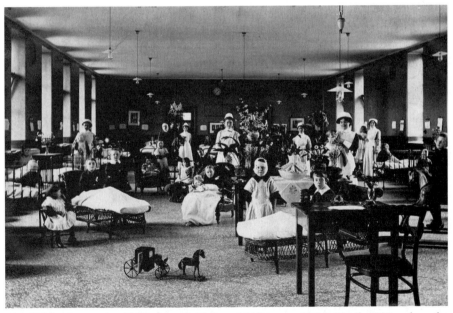

The children's ward, old Huddersfield Royal Infirmary, 1906. Until 1831, when the infirmary was opened, there was a dispensary in Pack Horse Yard. The medical officer received £20 per annum. In 1966 the building became part of Huddersfield Technical College. The infirmary is now at Lindley.

An exterior view of the infirmary. Those patients who weren't very ill probably enjoyed a better time at Christmas in the infirmary than they would have at home, especially if they were poor. Unveiled by King George on 11 July 1912, the building was said to have been considered by its builder, Joseph Kaye, 'the most handsome infirmary in England'.

The Sanatorium, Bradley Lane, 1911. 'M. Stevenson' wrote on the back of this card: 'the lady next to Dr Moore is your successor. We are having our wards painted. Huddersfield is as dull as ever, getting worse I think. Dr. Mac. hasn't got a post yet, and he is very sick. I think we are to be fixtures.' Patients in their beds used to be put out on verandahs – enough to kill them off rather than make them better, one might think.

Mill Hill Sanatorium, Dalton. This was built as an isolation hospital in the 1890s, and was where scarlet fever patients stayed until their infection had passed. The sanatorium was later used as an old people's home.

The typhoid fever ward, Mill Hill Sanatorium. Plenty of fresh air was allowed in through the open windows, while some ventured to sit outside, well wrapped up. It must have been windy – the lady on the right is keeping hold of her hat. The progress of patients used to be published in the *Huddersfield Examiner*, each identified by a number. When 'dangerously ill', a patient could be visited by relatives. 'Convalescent' meant that the patient was free from infection and awaiting discharge. A further classification was 'seriously ill but not in danger'. The newspaper was scanned eagerly every evening for patients' numbers.

St Luke's Hospital, Crosland Moor. At one time there was a workhouse nearby. Enjoying the grounds and a chat on the bench are four Huddersfield gentlemen. Abraham Townend is second from the right. He worked at Pat Martin's mill, Oakes.

The kitchen at Storthes Hall Asylum, Kirkburton, where some of the patients had to work. Relatives had to pay for them to stay at the asylum, and the journey there was a regular Saturday afternoon trek for many of those who visited. Unlike visitors to hospitals, they had little prospect that the patients would come out. So they made the best of things, and many friendships were formed on the buses to Kirkburton. When others are in the same boat it is so much easier to find something in common to talk about – and to laugh about.

SECTION THREE
Schools

Pupils at Birchencliffe. The huge rocking-horse at the back must have been a big incentive to go to school on Monday mornings, to see how 'Dobbin' was faring after the weekend.

Pupils of Paddock Council School. Miss Annie Whitworth taught at this school in the 1930s. In her bookcase photographs were found of this group of girls wearing tartan outfits. The occasion is unknown – Empire Day perhaps?

Another group of girls, this time in ship-shape form, from Paddock Council School.

Huddersfield Boys' College football team, 1928. Two full backs, Moorhouse and Jury, played in every match that season. That year Mr F. Haigh joined the college as handicraft master in place of Mr A.E. Baldick. Emmerson Bros of Brook's Yard, Market Street, was the oldest sports outfitters in town.

Pupils of Farnley Tyas School in the early 1900s. Stiff white collars, studs and even the odd bow-tie were the order of the day for the boys.

Prefects in Linthwaite School yard, 1937. Back row, left to right: Richard Gledhill, Harold Shaw, Norman Dearnley, Frank Townsend, Philip Whiteley. Middle rows include Evelyn Haigh, Dorothy Bamforth, Margaret Pogson, Jean Gilberthorpe, Doreen Wylde, Rene Smith, Sylvia Baker. Front row: Harold Norman, Geoff Shaw, Johnny Woodhead.

Pupils at Skelmanthorpe. In those days it was useless trying to play truant. Mothers would be at home washing and baking, blackleading the fireplace and attending to all of the other domestic chores. Neither were the children able to lose themselves in big departmental stores – there weren't any.

Pupils of King James's Grammar School, Aldmondbury, 1910. How smart the boys looked in uniform – and how easy to identify should they be guilty of any misdemeanour.

The front entrance hall, Municipal High School for Girls, Greenhead. One girl had the task of banging the gong, halfway up the staircase. It used to be sounded twice at dinnertime. For those girls who went home for dinner, it was a race to fly down those stairs and change into outdoor shoes to catch a trolley bus home – especially if the last period was a music lesson in the music room up at the top of another winding staircase.

Pupils of Deighton Council School. Miss Gothard, far left, is next to teacher Mr Hanson. Mr Colosme is on the far right. Mabel Priestley is fourth from the right in the third row back.

Deighton Council School pupils. Kenneth Brown is second from the right in the second row back. The teacher is thought to be Mr Armitage.

Pupils of Deighton Council School, 1927. Kenneth Brown is fourth from the left in the middle row. If teachers wanted silence they occasionally made children sit still with hands on their heads.

Board School and Baptist chapel, Oakes, 1907. To the right of the picture is a gas lamp. How exciting it was when the lamp lighter came round to light the lamps, which would cast an eerie pool of yellow light on autumn and winter nights.

Pupils at the rear of Birkby Council School, 1930s. The boys tended to keep to themselves – playing with girls was considered 'cissy'.

Crosland Moor schoolchildren, 1927. A long form was provided for boys. Back row, left to right: Keith Robinson, Eric Thornton, Harold Taylor, Denis Bradbury, Philip ?, Gilbert Wadsworth, Geoff Townend, Jack Jones, -?-, -?-, -?-. Second row includes: Kathleen Kirk, Marjorie Haigh, Hilda Riley, Doreen Rhodes, Dorothy Gibson, Ethel Avison. Front row includes: Queenie Smith, Helen Jamieson, Ruth Lister, Marjorie Kirkland.

Crosland Moor pupils, 1927. Remember when there was a 'window monitor' who had to deal with those pulleys when the windows needed to be opened or shut, and the consternation in summertime if a wasp or bee zoomed in? Note the ink-wells on the front desks – gone are the days of blotting-paper and huge ink blobs spoiling a previously pristine white page.

SECTION FOUR

Work

Joe Lancaster, family butcher, Moldgreen. These were the days when many had a joint on Sunday, cold meat and pickles with chips on Monday – something quick for wash-day – then the rest of the meat in a hotpot on Wednesday. Before refrigerators, meat safes were kept in cellars, with mesh across the front to keep out flies. Potted meat sandwiches, with plenty of Colman's mustard, was a tea fit for a king.

A group outside Deighton Sunday School. John Taylor of Deighton (with bald head and moustache) is in the centre. This was probably a wedding reception or funeral tea that was being catered for in the Sunday school. The photographer was Netherwood of Deighton.

Pat Martin's, Wellington Mills, c. 1930s. The building was all decked out to welcome King George V and Queen Mary on a visit to Huddersfield. The two gentlemen standing in the window on the far left look bent on committing suicide.

Employees of Pat Martin's. Abraham Townend is perched on the back of the bench, far left.

Employees of Huddersfield's first General Post Office. Before 1910 there were no ladies on the staff.

More employees of the first GPO. The building stands on an area once covered by green fields. The post office became Dugdale's.

The post office, Bradley. How pleasant it was to buy one's stamps at a pretty little stone post office such as this one. There's even a garden seat for shoppers to rest on. The 'Tea' sign on the wall suggests that it was either served or sold there.

Bradley and Colne Bridge Workingmen's Club. To refresh the body, if not the soul, a game of snooker or billiards was a common way for men to round off a busy weekday.

An unusual card to send for Christmas, 1914. The message 'With love to Gwen from Eveline' is written on the back. Employees of Huddersfield Confectionery Co., No. 15 Dundas Street, pose outside the premises. A sign for Fry's Chocolate is above the name of the firm in the middle window. The photograph must have been taken in the summertime, as two gentlemen are sporting straw boaters. All the men wear watch chains and 'Alberts' (watches) across their waistcoats. In their three-piece suits, collars and ties they all look extremely smart.

Horses and carts delivering goods outside the Three Nuns hostelry, Bradley. The horses are enjoying their lunch from nosebags, while a group of onlookers have forgotten the ale on the arrival of the photographer.

Eric Sutcliffe's new Jowett van, outside his greengrocers, Blacker Road, Fartown, 1937. Horses were still working at this time. Catherine's hairdressers is opposite.

Nigger, Blacker Road, 1949. Eric Sutcliffe's daughter, Veronica, wanted a horse, so Nigger became a regular sight in the area. His stable was in the back garden. The van had been sold in 1940.

A ceremony to mark the cutting of the first sod from B.H. Moxon and Son Ltd's new mill at Southfield, Kirkburton, 10 April 1948. Mrs Moxon holds the spade while Mr Matthew Moxon assists. Also present are managing director, Stanley Kinder, and the builder of the new mill, Mr Herbert Radcliffe. The decision to build a new factory was taken during the Second World War, but then delayed by the shortage of steel. The building was completed in two years. The single-storey premises occupied 60,000 square feet and incorporated 21,700 square feet of glass.

John L. Brierley. John started his company in two rooms at Commercial Mills, Firth Street, in 1893, when he was 22. In January 1901 the firm became a limited company called The Fancy Cotton Spinners Ltd, with directors John Brierley and Arthur Dawson. November 1912 saw it transferred back to Brierley as a private company. In 1903 the manufacture of elastic webbing began. In 1925 a mill in Quay Street was purchased and the standard working week was reduced from 55½ to 48 hours. Before and during the 1926 General Strike production at the mill was stopped owing to a lack of coal. Brierley's mill is one of the earliest examples in the town.

Shop Lane Mills, Kirkheaton. It must have been handy for a worker to live in a house which stood within a stone's throw of the mill – the siren could sound and he could be there in a minute.

Donald Gray, a blind Braille shorthand typist at Hopkinson's. Donald became blind in 1942, at the age of 14. He won second prize in his first baritone class competition at Mexborough in 1950, singing 'That God is Great'. He mastered Braille music in just three lessons, first playing the *Minuet in G* by J.S. Bach. His debut, in Huddersfield Town Hall on 12 December 1951, was at the annual Samuel Firth Christmas Party for the blind. After the tea he sang 'Silent Worship' by Handel and 'Sincerity' by Clarke. On 19 December 1958, pensioners of Hopkinson's held their annual dinner at the Ritz Café, and Donald provided the entertainment, accompanied at the piano by Conrad Jackson.

Watson Peel, his wife, Dorothy, and daughter, Beatrice. Peel owned a small mill in Skelmanthorpe opposite his home at No. 10 Spencer Street. With a partner he made rugs, curtains and those chenille-type tablecloths that were spread over tables when not in use. His daughter remains the proud owner of a pair of curtains and a crimson tassled cloth that he produced. Made in 1925, they are still better than many articles manufactured today. In the 1920s lots of little one-man businesses were set up. One, also in Skelmanthorpe, produced 'sacking' aprons, used for rough work. Peel died in 1927.

The shop between St Stephen's Terrace and Mount Street, Lockwood. One wonders what is more enchanting – a modern supermarket or advertisements for Sunlight soap, Cadbury's cocoa, Brooke Bond tea at 8d/quarter and tempting cakes in the window? The man in the doorway is looking business-like with his rolled-up sleeves, and probably a pencil above one ear for adding up the bill on a bit of paper.

F. France, grocer and confectioner, Towngate, Newsome. This was the era when potted meat was a regular at teatime and ham shanks were cooked slowly with mushy peas. I still have an order book of my dad's, written in 1922, when we had a village shop. With such items as Rinso at $3\frac{1}{2}$d, Beechams Powders 2d, butter $10\frac{1}{2}$d, yeast 3d and Bermaline 6d. Corned beef, sold loose, was sliced in the shop. Frequently customers left a balance, which never was paid off.

Neaverson's china shop, Byrom Street, 1937. In the doorway, left, is Kenneth Halstead. His wife, Winifred, worked there as a girl for the owner, Lewis Neaverson.

Harry Barrowclough, gardener, Oaklands, Dalton. Harry kept the garden belonging to this home for old ladies in tip-top condition. He could turn his hand to anything – even dry-stone walling. In 1990 the house became Oaklands Resource Centre, of the Kirklees Social Services.

Broadbent's coal wagon, having crashed into a parapet on a bridge. This mishap occurred sometime after the Second World War. Most of the coal was hurled into the river. With Hitler vanquished, the event provided something else to talk about.

Leisure

The boating lake, Hope Bank Pleasure Gardens, Honley. In those days a holiday often meant a day out at the pleasure gardens. Why travel further, especially if, as the writer of this postcard declared, there were 'plenty of girls'? What could be nicer than a sunny day, a picnic lunch, boating, dancing and plenty of other amusements, plus the delightful surrounding countryside? Philip Walker even remembered skating at Hope Bank in the moonlight.

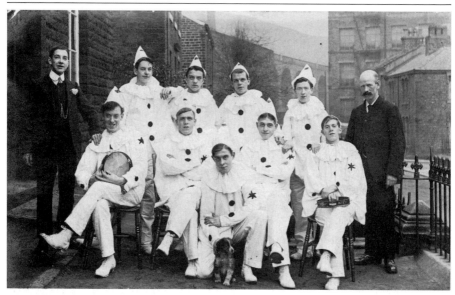

Slaithwaite Methodist Star Pierrots. The sweet little dog, centre, seems to be looking for his costume.

Moldgreen Congregational Church Gypsy Choir. What fun it must have been to dress up in colourful outfits and bang those tambourines, perhaps after a monotonous day's work in a mill or factory.

Members of the Deighton Working Men's Club, blacked up for a concert.

Huddersfield Theatre Royal staff, outside the Victoria Inn, 1904. What a loss to the town it was when the theatre closed down in 1961. Going to the theatre was even more of an occasion than going to the picture house. Many famous actors and actresses graced the boards, including Ivor Novello in *The Rat* in March 1924. The musical comedy *No, No, Nanette* was on in November 1926, and the week before saw the play *The Last of Mrs Cheyney*. In spring 1927 a mannequin parade was held in the Theatre Royal, admission to which was by invitation card only.

F.K. Harburn of No. 3 Sufton Street, Birkby. For summer outings what better than a group of friends going on a charabanc trip? Mr Harburn had a 'chara' and advertised 'For joyous outings, try the "vindictive superbe" coach'. Such *bonhomie* was generated by an 'open-to-the-sky chara to Paradise', even if it was only going to Blackpool on a day-trip.

A cricket match, Fartown, 1920s. Pleasure and dignity combined to make these occasions supreme. Everybody dressed up, there's not a bare head in sight, and good behaviour was the normal way of living.

Members of Huddersfield Postcard Society in the Public Library, celebrating Mrs Marion Barrowclough's eightieth birthday, February 1980. Marion is in the centre, Granville and Hazel Wheeler (the author) are to her right. Duncan Carter is on the far left, George Wolstenholme is in front of the exit sign (wearing spectacles) and Fred Hepworth is to his left. Marion founded the Postcard Society, and she was one of the original Bamforth child models on song cards prior to the First World War.

Cambridge Road Baths. Dancing and big bands will live for ever in the memory of those lucky enough to have attended the Baths, especially during the Second World War. Billy Hobson, organist, who played at the Ritz Cinema, occasionally entertained here. Marjorie Stanley smiles out of the happy crowd, standing next to the tall gentleman in the suit and tie.

Presentation of the bowling cup to Allen Hirst, 15 July 1966. Allen was the work study officer at Brook Motors. With him are Howard Bradley, general manager of Brook Motors, and Brian Cook.

Muriel Kelly, Chris Searle and Della, 1979. Muriel was a singer and ex-member of Huddersfield Choral Society. She was due to appear on TV's *That's Life*, not for her singing but because of Della, her 'singing dog'. To make sure that she sang on cue when the television people arrived in Hepworth, Muriel insisted that Della should practise every day. Alas, on the big day, when Chris Searle, the interviewer, arrived, the dog's voice was a mere croak – her moment of TV fame wasn't to be. However, many people will recall Muriel's beautiful singing voice, and that of Della, whose top notes were something to be marvelled at.

Herman Barker. Herman joined Huddersfield and Colne Valley Physical Culture Club in Milnsbridge when he was 13. Over the years he won twenty-eight gold and silver medals and several trophies, and in 1934 he became the wrestling champion of Yorkshire at his weight. His mother played the piano at Slaithwaite Picture House in the days of the silent movie. Herman bought a guitar for 12s 6d and later joined the Noranda Banjo, Mandoline and Guitar Orchestra, which performed concerts for hospitals and charities.

Huddersfield Town Association Football Club, 1920s or '30s. This was a time when Saturday afternoon at the football match was the treat at the weekend for the men. Meanwhile their wives went shopping in town, getting home in time to provide a hearty tea for their husbands and sons, who had been cheering themselves hoarse on the terraces. Their team winning or losing the match made or marred many people's weekends.

Clayton West Brass Band, 1917. George Gray (see Introduction), the father of Donald (see p. 45), is the flugal horn player second from the right in the front row. He worked in Springwood Colliery and claimed that his greatest achievement was in promoting the pit-head baths, for which workers paid a penny a week.

Ernest Cooper, Huddersfield Town Hall organist. For many years Ernest was the accompanist to the Huddersfield Choral Society.

Donald Gray and others who competed in another singing competition, 1953. Alan Graham from Honley won the rose bowl that day. The following day Donald, far left, won the operatic section for bass baritone. Although blind, Donald is one of the most cheerful people one could hope to meet. His wife, Dorothy, prefers reading to him, rather than watching a television set. Few fully sighted people ever look as happy as Donald. His secret stems largely from a love of good music, and, he says, 'the spiritual light'.

All set for an outing from Folly Hall. The three older ladies look a little dubious. With their backs to the driver they wouldn't know if they were still attached to the horse, which appears to have an extra short tail!

Transport a bit more advanced has been arranged for this party from Lepton. According to the note on the back of the card, the passengers are 'Father, Gwen, Norah, Dorothy, Kathleen'. 'Father' resembles the driver of the horse and carriage in the previous photograph. All are taking the outing very seriously.

A solitary lady on Lindley Moor. On 20 August 1924 the sender of this postcard wrote: 'We went to these moors last Monday and was nearly blown away. The heather is in flower.'

Enoch Hutton, the uncle of the famous cricketer, Len, instructs Girl Guides in using a telephone. Few people owned a private telephone in the 1920s and '30s.

Enoch Hutton and Boy Scouts. It was in January 1908 that Robert Baden-Powell's book, *Scouting for Boys*, was published in fortnightly parts and Scout troops began to spring up all over the country. He called them a 'great friendly brotherhood', all dressed alike and with the same aim: to make themselves, through scout training, into healthy, happy, helpful citizens of their country.

Elderly residents of Fernside, Aldmondbury, off on an outing. Mrs Jenny Ellison is second from the left. Her pug dog, Yogi, was also a well-known figure. There were prefab buildings at Aldmondbury prior to the flats and bungalows of the 1960s (seen in the background).

A policeman enjoying a bite to eat, watched by an envious dog. They are both at the filming site of *Last of the Summer Wine*, Forest Road, Dalton.

Snowtime in Greenhead Lane, Dalton, January 1984. The snow is being enjoyed by Granville Wheeler, far right, and local boys.

A concert at an unknown location. A Deighton lady gave this picture to me years ago. She thought it depicted a concert given by the Sunday school, coached by John Edward Varley. There never used to be time for youngsters to complain of boredom: there were concert rehearsals to attend, Sunday school, playing out, and running errands for those who couldn't get to the shops themselves.

SECTION SIX

Events

Hinchliffe Mill Industrial Society wagon and horses with a load of youngsters, all dressed up and ready to go. Big events were usually connected with Sunday school, Co-op and works outings before sophisticated holidays abroad became common.

Skelmanthorpe Co-op centenary celebrations, 1934. Everybody came out to stand and stare. Fish and meat pastes are advertised in the windows, and Crysella soap flakes on the wagon. The only sign to pull onlookers down to earth was: 'P. Horwich, Dentist', on the far right.

General William Booth, founder of the Salvation Army, draws the crowds at Denby Dale, July 1907. Visits from notable people inspired multitudes to turn out.

St Patrick's church garden party, Greenhead Hall, 7 July 1900.

Nurses marching in Milnsbridge Nurses' Fête, 7 July 1906.

Nurses' Carnival, St George's Square, 16 June 1909. The square is thronged with onlookers. Some had vantage seats in windows, including those of J.W. & H. Shaw, woollen manufacturers, next to the Huddersfield Building Society. James Watkinson & Sons, next to Cobden Hotel, is at the top right.

Musical Festival, Longwood, 13 August 1905. This was known as the Longwood Sing. It is odd how it always seemed to shine on the righteous in those days, and picture hats could be worn without a gale tearing them off heads.

Lascelles Hall Cricket Club Carnival, 17 July 1909. The float belonged to Whitworth Bros, who sold hay, corn and straw.

Gentlemen's outing, Honley. John Theaker's wagonette provides the transport. Don't they look debonair? Oh, for a return of those fashions, especially the straw boaters and wide-brimmed trilby hats.

Fartown Trinity Wesleyan Band of Hope float, Whit Tuesday, 1911. This won first prize.

Members of Milton Church Band of Hope, Whit Tuesday, 1913.

Huddersfield's 25,000 candle power illuminated coronation car, 22 June 1911. All that splendour is set against the sombre backdrop of a gas lamp, mill chimneys and terraced houses blackened with soot.

Pupils at New Street, Milnsbridge, 1916. These girls won second prize in the Mrs Sunderland Musical Competition.

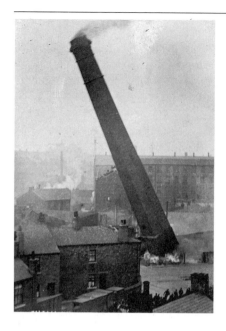

A chimney being demolished at Deadwaters, 6 July 1909.

General Rundle leaving the Huddersfield Drill Hall, 30 June 1906. This postcard was sent from a Pte H. Hellawell, G Company, Ninth Fusiliers, Fort William, Calcutta. The poster on the left asks for recruits for all branches of His Majesty's Army. The stone beneath it was laid by Lord Roberts of Kandahar. I wonder whether the small boys watching wished they were old enough to join up.

Rolls of Honour. After the fighting and glory came the reckoning and scenes like this were common all over the country. The vehicle on the left belonged to Sharp's Transport. A Mrs Dwyer and family of No. 7 Freshold Street, Primrose Hill, wrote on the back of the postcard to a Mrs Clegg: 'Thanks for P.C. Glad to hear you are having a good time and nice weather. The weather is broke at home. Mrs Hirst wishes to be remembered to you. I am feeling grand just now thank God. It feels nice to be able to do a little bit of something to make it a bit lighter for Mary.'

The wedding of George Vernon Baxter (solicitor) and Elsie Whittaker, 10 August 1921.

Holmfirth tradesmen's outing, 1928. This joyful occasion included wives, children and the children's grandparents.

Hanson's coaches and Holmfirth tradesmen, ready for an outing, 1928.

Thornton Lodge Methodist choir trip, 1928. Charabanc trips were made all the jollier by those taking part singing hymns and songs of the 1920s, such as 'Sing as we go, and let the world go by', which was popularized by Gracie Fields. Note the daredevil at the back of the vehicle.

The programme for the English Cup Final, Huddersfield Town v. Preston North End, 1922. The train left Huddersfield station, from the top end, at 8.15 a.m. and lunch on the train was at midday. On arrival at Marylebone luggage was left at the headquarters – the Great Central Hotel. Motor charabancs left the hotel at 1.45 p.m. for the kick-off at 3.00 p.m. Dinner at the Great Central Hotel was at 6.45 p.m. On Sunday 30 April breakfast was at 9.30 a.m. The train departed from Marylebone at 11.15 a.m. and lunch on the train was at 1.00 p.m. On arrival at Penistone, at 3.23 p.m., motor conveyances met the party to take them to St George's Square. On the programme, ladies and gentlemen were requested to note that times would be strictly adhered to, and those not in their places would be left behind.

HUDDERSFIELD TOWN FOOTBALL CLUB.

ENGLISH CUP FINAL

v.

Preston North End.

SATURDAY, April 29th, 1922,

AT

Stamford Bridge Ground,
CHELSEA.

Programme of Arrangements.

The centenary of Clayton West High Street Methodist church, 1934. In those days there were eight churches and chapels in the area.

Donald Gray of No. 10 Spencer Street, Skelmanthorpe. When he was 40, Donald went completely blind. It didn't deter him from enjoying life and winning numerous singing competitions. A bass-baritone, he was employed at Hopkinson's, Birkby, as a Braille shorthand typist. On 1 June 1956 he won the rose bowl at Lytham St Anne's – just one of the many musical festivals that have been delighted by his singing.

Skelmanthorpe Male Voice Choir, 1949. Dorothy Peel is sixth from the left in the front row. She accompanied both the choir and her husband-to-be, Donald Gray, at the piano. They were married on 20 April 1963. The guest singer here was the soprano Gwen Catley. Back row, left to right: Bobby Peel, Willie Green, Frank Thornton, Stanley Thornton, Willie Thornton, John Littlewood, Edward Taylor, Albert Senior, Donald Heywood, Terence Morley, Cecil Taylor. Second row: Fred Biltcliffe, George Ferguson, Tom Radley, Harry Shaw, Ernest Allsop, Reggie Ellam, Wilfred Thompson, R. Mallinson, Stewart Gill, Willie Morley, Arthur Peel, Charles Barrowclough. Front row: Herbert Gray, Jimmy Eden (who hawked sewing requisites, dusters, etc.), Guy Burton, Cecil Lodge, Leslie Kendall (conductor), Dorothy Peel, Gwen Catley, Ernest Cooper (organist), Willie Derbyshire, Percy Wragg, Frank Horn, Frank Radley.

The Princess Royal, Mary, and her husband, the Earl of Harewood, in Holmfirth, 5 August 1927. On the left there are some nurses, in case anyone is overcome by the occasion.

The Co-op Choir wins a shield, c. 1960s. Ronnie Daniels was the choir master. Joan Donaldson is seventh from the left in the middle row. She has enjoyed the companionship of a number of guide dogs and is a well-known figure in the town. On her left is Hilda Gregory (née Taylor), of the grocer's shop at Deighton.

Colne Valley Male Voice Choir Golden Jubilee Concert, May 1972. The conductor is John Gulley. The choir combined with the Yorkshire Concert Orchestra on this occasion. Norman Dearnley is sixth from the left in the back row. He began singing when he was seven in Linthwaite church choir. In the Second World War he sang 'Song of Songs' on the All India Radio Forces Network. He was taught by George Stead, a professional singing teacher. Still in Huddersfield Choral Society and now in his seventies, he frequently sings solos in Linthwaite church.

An unexpected flood, Bay Hall, Birkby, 30 May 1937.

The laying of the foundation stone of Skelmanthorpe Liberal Club. The mills and factories of the area were the cornerstone of many working lives, and a trip down to 't' club' for a game of billiards or snooker and a pint took care of the evening for the men.

The wedding of Donald Gray to Dorothy Peel, 20 April 1963. Donald's great-grandfather, Joseph Pickles, played the organ at Clayton West Congregational church for forty years until 1903. He had a post-horn and played the trumpet obligato in York Minster for Mrs Sunderland (see p. 69). Mr Pickles made himself a set of wooden teeth so that he could continue playing the post-horn, often heard on the stage-coach. Donald loved to hear stories about him on homeward journeys across fields after entertaining Lord Allendale with his post horn at Bretton Hall.

Mr R. Dugald Monteith, doctor, of Longley Road, Huddersfield. On his election pamphlet in 1956 he told people: 'We have a share of the Exchequer Equalisation Grant worth a 3s rate. The new rate of 17s 6d represents a fair and true rate to meet essential needs.' A start had been made to replace old slum dwellings and improve housing standards, and he wished to see the expansion of the technical college.

People

The Baxter family. Left to right: George, Annie, Gerald, Edie and William. Baxter, Caulfield are well-known solicitors in the town.

George Baxter, looking smart in uniform during the First World War.

Abraham Townend and his wife, Emma, the grandparents of Geoffrey Townend. The couple lived at Quarmby Fold and had three sons and one daughter, but Abraham died before his youngest son was born. Vincent Hatch of Huddersfield was the photographer.

John Kenneth Halstead, born 16 June 1905, with his mother, Mabel Rachel Halstead, and his grandma, photographed at Netheroyd. Mabel was a talented artist and Kenneth later became a keen photographer, employed at Hopkinson's, Birkby.

Councillor Albert Rookes Halstead and Mrs Mabel Halstead, the parents of Kenneth and Margaret. As well as being married, Albert and Mabel were cousins.

'Grandma Whiteley' of Quarmby, Geoff Townend's 'gran'ma'. She smoked a long clay pipe and brewed beer, which was put in a bowl and placed on flagstones to cool. In the corner of the hearth there was a quaint metal jar that contained her tobacco. She died in 1914 at the age of 90.

Emma Whiteley in her youth. One hardly expected such frivolous behaviour in those days!

A couple of pretty 1920s bright young things – Margaret Halstead (seated) and Winifred, her sister-in-law. The latter, married to Kenneth, worked in Neaverson's china shop on Byrom Street and later ran the arts and crafts shop on the same street. Margaret married Clifford Chesters and lived at Bradley Bar, later retiring to Whitby.

A group of girls walking at Wessenden, 1928. In the 1920s many youngsters were obsessed with the great outdoors, and none more so that Winifred Halstead (far right) and Muriel Cheetham (far left), later Mrs Tom Jessop of Deighton.

Party time for Carol Halstead (second row, far right) and friends, *c.* 1949. Carol attended Greenhead High School, which is now a mixed sixth form college.

A splashing time for Brian Halstead and friends. Brian was a pupil at Huddersfield Boys' College. Remember those elasticated swimming costumes and tightly fitting caps? Will she or won't she dash that bucket of water over one of them?

Ian Clelland and Chummy at No. 19 Leafield Close, Sheepridge. The No. 10 trolley bus for Sheepridge is on the left. Ian used to be a 'Saturday boy', ringing the bell on buses and earning 5s for three hours' work.

Hazel Taylor (later Wheeler) and Major, Deighton Road, 1948. We lived at the village shop, where Major often sat behind the counter. I worked at the Halifax Building Society at one time, and before that I was an art student at Huddersfield Technical College. The only writing I did at this time was my diary and letters to boyfriends in the services. Every day has been recorded in diaries since!

Owners of Deighton Central Stores. John Taylor is second from the left in the back row. Jane Taylor is on the far left. John's brother, Law Taylor, is second from the right in the back row. He was Mayor of Huddersfield three times during the 1920s. The occasion was a garden party in the market garden in Deighton, which was owned by Richard Taylor.

Herman Barker and other members of the RAF, 1943. Herman is second from the right. In 1942 he was posted to Cornwall at the time when *Love Story* was being filmed there, for which the theme music was *Cornish Rhapsody*. He was one of three hundred extras, and was paid £3 a day for three days. He didn't manage to see the film since he was posted overseas before it was released. Recently Herman finally saw the film, which was in the archives of the Bradford Playhouse. It was arranged for him to have a private viewing. He recognized himself in one of the crowd scenes, and said it was 'eerie to see himself as a young man again'. John Crowther's mill paid his wife £1 5s weekly throughout the war years, also sending Herman £5 a month as 'spending money'.

Louie, Polly, Herman, Elsie and Nora Barker, all wearing clogs.

Geoffrey Townend, outside his house in Hawthorne Terrace, Crosland Moor, August 1922. His family kept livestock and once sold a goose, which used to grab hold of Geoffrey's mother's pinny and drag her round. The goose was carried to another home in Pymroyd, but by the time the person who had carried it there arrived back home, it had flown back too.

Bessie Hellewell (later Mrs Townend), 1942.
After Greenhead High School, Bessie worked
in the buying office at United Threadmills.
Geoffrey and Bessie Townend now live in
Holmfirth.

The 'Huddersfield Eccentric', who has had
many titles, including Jake Jonathon
Zebedee Mangle Wurzel and Longwood
Singh. His dog, Manoyle, rides proudly in
the basket on the back of his bike. Wurzel
has been featured on a television
programme about eccentric people.

Working girls on their lunch hour, 1930s. Left to right: Hilda Williams, Elsie Ogden, Marjorie Stanley (Hilda's sister). They all worked at Universal Stores. Hilda, from Sheepridge, is wearing fashionable gauntlet gloves.

Marjorie Williams (later Mrs Jack Stanley). When Marjorie worked at Universal Stores her employer sent in this photograph of her for a modelling competition. Whether or not she won, she ought to have! Marjorie and Jack later ran a butcher's shop in Cowlersley.

Marjorie and Jack Stanley with a friend,
Madge Preston (in the side-car), on holiday
in Blackpool, 1930s.

All girls together at Universal Stores. Left to
right: Marjorie Williams (later Mrs Stanley),
Elsie Newton, Doris Quarmby, Bessie
Robinson.

Enoch and Hannah Bottom of Holly Bank Road, Lindley. Enoch was a wheelwright and died in 1892.

Boy Scout Eric Sutcliffe, who was in the 48th Lindley Wesleyans. He paid 1d a week subscription and 3d toward the uniform. In later years he became Group Scoutmaster at Holy Trinity, Marsh, and owned the greengrocers in Blacker Road (see p. 43).

Eric's daughter, Veronica, trying out a friend's horse outside the family shop on Blacker Road.

Rosie Coletta and Jimmy Hirst. Coletta's is a well-known name in Huddersfield. Oh, those delicious twopenny ice-cream cornets of the 1930s! Coletta's had a café in Westgate, Huddersfield.

Mildred Sutcliffe, on the right, shows off baby Veronica, in between a bit of washing, to a neighbour in the yard between Blacker Road and Nursery Street. They appear as happy as larks, despite there being a war on.

Members of Huddersfield Authors' Circle visit Hilda Gledhill and Halifax writers in Barkisland, August 1981. The second row includes, from the left: Pauline Murray, Hazel Wheeler, Mildred Coldwell, and Edward Adkins, second on the right, formerly a journalist for the *Huddersfield Examiner*. Front row: Cynthia Hand, Hilda Gledhill, Marjorie Wilkinson, Muriel Kelly, Joyce Woodhouse. The canine contributor to the seminar was Della, Muriel's 'Singing Schnauzer' (see p. 55).

Hilda Taylor and niece, Carol Halstead, in the henyard at the back of Central Stores, Deighton, during the Second World War. In the background is the council school. Hilda is wearing a pair of dungarees. It was still a rarity for girls to wear trousers in the 1940s, but they were useful for 'digging for victory' in the back garden.

Cissie Ferguson (far right) with friends Nan and Elsie, 1922. Cissie was a schoolteacher and was a friend of another teacher, Annie Whitworth. Though having up to forty pupils in a class, they managed to keep discipline without any bother. Cissie married Brook Dews and lived in Blackmoorfoot Road, Crosland Moor.

Mr C.H. Avison of No. 16 Hawthorne Terrace, Crosland Moor, 1906. He was a commercial traveller in textiles.

Elizabeth Wheeler's twelfth birthday party in the garden at Greenhead Lane, Dalton, 4 May 1966. Elizabeth is in the centre at the front, her sister, Caroline, is standing on the right, eating a brandy snap, and Carolyn Jackson is just behind Elizabeth, to the left. The two girls wearing hairbands were Hungarian and also attended Dalton Junior School before emigrating to Australia. Hilda Gregory (formerly Taylor) of Central Stores, Deighton (before moving to Cowlersley), is officiating. One could usually rely on 4 May being warm enough to enjoy a picnic outside.

SECTION EIGHT

Worship

Buxton Road chapel. This photograph was sent to Mrs J. Lord of No. 123 Oak Street, Elland, on 28 May 1904. This was an era when it was normal for everyone, young and old and in-betweens, to worship on Sunday in chapel or church, or simply to read the Bible at home if they were unable to venture out.

A horse and cart passing St Thomas's church, Longroyd Bridge.

Deighton chapel in its heyday, before the left side of the churchyard had even been used for graves.

St Barnabas church, Crosland Moor, 1908. It is a long time since one heard the mooing of cows here. Opposite is David Brown Park Works.

The Wesleyan church, Hillhouse. This was commonly known as 'Tea Pot Chapel'. What would the gentleman in the bowler hat and Sunday best have said had he known that, in years to come, the chapel would be converted into a mosque?

Linthwaite church. In the 1930s the choirboys here rebelled against wearing stiff white collars with studs. When asked to attend and sing at the wedding of a local solicitor, Leonard Bamforth, the choirboys secretly pushed the studs down a grate in the church aisle, refusing to wear them again until it was agreed to increase the choirboys' fee. Revd Pobjoy was the vicar in the 1930s.

Linthwaite Church Prize Choir, 1922. Back row, left to right: Lewis Bamforth, -?-, Herman Shaw, Harry Knight, -?-, Frank Gaunt, Francis Dyson, -?-, -?-, Harry Chadwick. Second row: -?-, -?-, Lesley Clay, Alfred Knight, George Lockwood, -?-, -?-, John Pickles. Third Row: Herman Barker, -?-, ? Chadwick, -?-, Gledhill Sykes (choir master), -?-, -?-, -?-, -?-. Front row: -?-, Jack Whiteley, -?-, -?-, Harry Jackson, Carl Pownall.

The original Deighton Sunday School. Law Taylor's house is on the far left. Note the nosey parkers peering out of the windows of the Sunday school. When the later Deighton Sunday School closed down, the building housed a business selling windows and glass.

Districts

Haymakers at Linthwaite, viewed from Blackmoorfoot. Linthwaite church is in the distance. The workman on the right is holding what appears to be a stone bottle – perhaps one of those containing ginger beer.

Harvest time. What fun it was to ride atop a pile of hay carried by a horse and cart, and to leap into smaller haystacks.

The railway line from Huddersfield to Meltham, which ran alongside the entrance to Beaumont Park. It must have been a fascinating vantage point for the boys sitting on top of the bridge, but a bit precarious with their legs over the edge.

Paddock Foot, 1904. On the left is the Talbot Hotel, on the corner of Colne Street. The licensee used to be Rosana Haigh. The Plough Boy Inn was on the opposite side of the road. Both have since been demolished.

Longroyd Bridge. J. Schofield, a printer, is on the left, advertising the Great Ebor horse race. Zebra grate polish is advertised on the tram and there are Colman's starch and Players Navy Cut cigarettes signs on the left. Springwood School is in the centre background and St Thomas's church is on the right.

Cows at Skelmanthorpe.

This postcard was posted to Miss Bertha Allan of Thurlstone Bank, near Penistone, on 14 September 1905. The news was that Mrs Joe Walker's baby was dead and that they were having nice weather. The Boot and Shoe Inn is on the right.

These almost identical houses in Leeds Road have similar net curtains at the windows. The post office and parcel depot is towards the right. This view was taken by the photographer Netherwood of Deighton.

Brook Street, Moldgreen, 1904. The car registration number is CX 149. Differences from today include the driver's highly polished tall silk hat and the gas lamps. How reassuring those chimneys look – no need to fear a power cut in those days, when homely curls of smoke poured from the chimneys on cold winter nights.

The Baths, Kirkheaton, 1904. In those days when not every household possessed a bath, it is not clear whether these premises were for swimming or taking a bath. Telephones, too, were a novelty for the average household.

The tramcar to Slaithwaite, coming up Whiteley Bottom, Milnsbridge, 1904. This was the day of the Yorkshire Show in Huddersfield. The message on the back of this postcard reads: 'All going fairly straight over here till this a.m. Shafting strained bottom room new mill, stopped for today at least, everybody going to show. Got about ¾ of wages done already.' Zebra grate polish is advertised on the front of the tram.

St John's Road, Birkby, August 1905. A hive of industry surrounds this peaceful scene: at Clare Hill were Alfred Jubb & Sons' printing works, Nelson & Woolger, the merchant shippers, and Wallaces Ltd, the grocers; Moulden & Co., shipping merchants, and Thomas S. Wallis & Co., woollen merchants, were in Cambridge Road; opposite St John's Road were the offices and works at Bay Hill of Shaw's pale dry ginger ale and hop ale, 'the premier non-intoxicants'.

Thunderbridge, 1907. 'Mabel' wrote on the back of this pretty woodland view: 'Mother will be coming down on Saturday afternoon, but not to stay. She will shop first. Will you get a loaf. She will bring some eggs. Glad to hear you are both improving.' How much simpler it was to cater for guests in those days, without all the palaver of starters and so on. No wonder people were able to manage on small wages, yet seemed contented – a walk in the woods, bread and butter and a boiled egg for tea. Heaven!

Birkby Hall Road, 1908. If only we could wave a magic wand and somehow transport ourselves back in time to the peaceful, calm way of life pictured here. Imagine being able to wake up and look out of one of those cottage windows in Edwardian Huddersfield.

Tram Terminus, Crosland Moor.

The tram terminus, Crosland Moor, 1908. There was no problem waiting for transport then in those lovely little weather-proof shelters.

Westbourne Road, Marsh. On the left is H.D. Green's shop and next to it is S. Shaw. The West End Pharmacy, Armitage Chemist, is opposite. In 1924 a millinery business at No. 63 Westbourne Road, Marsh, was for sale, the rent for which was 10s 6d a week, including rates.

Children playing around The Old Hall, Shepley, 1909. The pencilled message on the back of the picture postcard reads: 'If it is fit on Tuesday night, Nance and I are coming down to the Park, either by the 6.30 or 6.50 from here. Will you come to meet us for an hour or so, but don't forget to bring Meg. Clifford has been in bed a day last week, but he is better.'

Trees in full leaf in Stone Wood, Shepley, August 1906. The message on this card was not as flourishing: 'Dear Edith, Hannah may as well stay the week, as I am no worse but not much better. Clifford is in bed poorly. The doctor says it is his spine that is very weak. I am better of the sickness.'

Berry Brow station, 1910. This was part of the LNWR Penistone and Sheffield line. On the right there were stone carvings of trains leaving a tunnel, one of which is preserved in Ravensknowle Museum.

Brockholes Junction. Clarence posted this card to a friend in Blackpool in August 1911. He was glad she was having a 'jolly time', and wished he was there with her.

Cock o' Farnley, Huddersfield.

Cock o'Farnley, 1911. On 11 May 1904 there had been cock fighting at Farnley and magistrates imposed fines on those involved.

Outlane post office, kept by Joe Haigh. This was also a grocer, tobacconist and an agency for the West End Laundry.

The black dog on the right hand side, outside the shop advertising Lyons tea, Rowntrees chocolates and Fry's cocoa, must have had an interesting life watching the trams go by. Nearby was a track leading into Pat Martin's, Wellington Mills, Oakes, for the conveyance of coal by truck from the centre of town at Hillhouse sidings.

Woodhouse Avenue, Fartown. Mr and Mrs Joe Wood and their daughter, Jeanne, used to live at No. 29. Joe worked at Hopkinson's, Birkby. In 1927 The West Riding Furnishing Co. of Nos 79–81 King Street, Huddersfield, encouraged people to 'own a home of your own, for 30 pennies a week'. The lady at the gate, wearing a mob-cap and long skirt, looks the type to revel in owning one of these well-built houses.

Central Avenue, Fartown. The three ladies outside the shop may be contemplating some Lyons ice-cream, which is advertised on the left. This was a desirable area in which to live – not too far from town yet close to the countryside.

Lodge Row, Aldmondbury Bank, 1910. Every house has a chimney, which was more work than modern central heating, but far more cosy.

Barton Road, Crosland Moor. The men are seated outside Fred Walker's pub. Barton Road is now Blackmoorfoot Road.

A full-flowing river under Somerset Bridge, August 1922. On the back of this postcard 'Clara' wrote to 'Alice': 'Hope the weather will take up for you, we have had three bad days.' The horse-drawn vehicle on the bridge is advertising Van Houten's cocoa and Bovril.

Newhouse Hall, alongside Newhouse Wood, 1922. I wish friends would send postcards of local scenes today, because it's not so easy to keep a telephone call! The message on this card reminded Mr D. Armitage that the writer was going to meet her father at Canker Lane by the waiting-room on Saturday.

Grove Corner, Skelmanthorpe, *c.* 1930s. The cluster of village shops on the left includes Wallaces.

A tramcar, New Hey Road, Salendine Nook, 1930s. The schoolboys would have played very different games from these enjoyed today. In 1932 Rushworth's in Huddersfield had a diabolo demonstration: 'The devil on two sticks – see the expert diabolo player, 10 a.m. – 1 p.m. and 2 p.m. – 5 p.m. on the second floor.' Many boys collected tram tickets and rolled marbles down the tram lines. One of the buildings on the right was Salendine Nook post office.

The village, Newsome. Uttleys High Class Fisheries is on the left. Before the Second World War 'a fish and a pennorth', from the local 'chip hole', was often the staple dinnertime diet of many. They tasted better than ever from a newspaper – usually the *Examiner* – on a cold and frosty evening after going to the pictures.

Oaklands Home for the Elderly, Greenhead Lane, Dalton, 1960s. It has become Oaklands Resource Centre (see p. 48). The top lawn became a car park and in 1993 building began at the lower and top sides of the old house.

Waingate, Berry Brow, 1965. Smoke is furling out of chimneys merrily, before the era of smokeless zones.

Greenhead Lane, Dalton, with the old coach house lodge. When Susan Richardson lived there, she was washing one Monday morning and thought she saw a small girl, whom she supposed to be her young daughter, who had gone to school. Then the vision vanished. An old lady who used to live at the lodge told Mrs Richardson that a little girl had died in the corn barn of the house – which was now the bathroom, where the vision had been seen. Years ago the lodge was demolished, in order to widen the lane. When new houses are built there, I wonder if any of the residents will see a ghost of about nine, with shoulder-length, fair hair and an intent gaze?

Acknowledgements

Special thanks are due to Mr Bill Exley for generously allowing me to borrow many pictures from his collection. Many thanks go to Mr and Mrs Donald Gray. Donald will not see this book, but will derive great pleasure from his wife, Dorothy, reading to him.

Thanks are due to Mr and Mrs Geoff Townend, Mrs Mary Allison, Mr and Mrs David Whitworth, Mr Herman Barker, Mrs Marjorie Stanley, Mr Norman Dearnley and Mr Richard Heath and the *Huddersfield Examiner*.

Thanks for the loan of photographs must also go to Mr Brian Halstead, Mrs O. Clelland, Mrs Lena McManus and Mr Allen Hirst.

When moving to a new house it is so easy to throw away old photographs, letters and other ephemera. Please don't – they are the substance that connects us to our past.

This is one of the most popular forms of Amusement at Huddersfield Come here and do likewise.

Fashions alter, but amusements remain the same when spring is in the air and a young man's fancy turns to thoughts of love.